Reflections

of the Heart

By Rose Gingerich

This book is dedicated to Jesus Christ, my Lord and Savior. He paid a debt I could not pay. I owe Him so much and desire to serve Him with my life. These poems are **Reflections** of my heart as I meditate on God and His great love for us. His Word has been powerful in my life and an inspiration for these poems as well. God has inspired me to write these thoughts and reflections in poem form. He has been my Rock and Jesus my Redeemer through many rough roads. I could not have written these without the Spirit to lead me. So I want to thank God the Father, God the Son, and the Holy Spirit for making this possible. My prayer is that someone, somewhere might be touched by these **Reflections**, and that my life and my poems would shine in such a way that Christ is portrayed. I also thank you, the reader, and ask that God would richly bless you as you read. If these bless you, please pass one along to a friend or someone who might need a blessing.

In Christ,
Rose

Contents

Life Reflections

May my heart be made complete
As I sit low at Jesus' feet.
May my soul find sweet rest
Knowing I am truly blessed.
May my spirit be set free
By the truth You've given to me.
May my eyes focus on You
As I remain ever true.
May my lips proclaim good news
Showing others the way to choose.
May my feet walk in Your Way
And keep me from going astray.
May my ears listen for Your voice
As I seek You to make my choice.
May my life reflect what's inside it
And may I never try to hide it.

God's Masterpiece

At the end of the day
The sun begins to descend
God pulls out His paints
With brushes in His hand
The canvas is stretched across the sky
As He begins the great Masterpiece
With just one stroke of His hand
He turns the sky a brilliant red
Then with a touch of purple
And a tint of bright pink hues
The Masterpiece comes alive
As the last light fades away
I stand and gaze in awe
At the Masterpiece God has made
I can tell it's an original
It was signed by His hand
No one else could even come close
To creating a Masterpiece like this.

A New Day Dawns

As I thank the Lord
For another new day
The first light of dawn appears
And I thank the Lord
For eyes to behold it's beauty
The first birds begin to sing
And I thank the Lord
That I have ears to hear
I smell fresh coffee brewing
And I thank the Lord
That I'm able to smell
As I pour my first cup
The cup warms my cold hands
And I thank the Lord
For the sense of touch
I bite into a yummy sweet roll
And I thank the Lord
That I can taste and enjoy it
I know this will be another good day
For the Lord has given me so much

Freedom

Freedom is a bird let out of its cage
Or an old man released from this age.
It's like a blind man receiving his sight
Or from darkness, stepping into the light.

Freedom is a butterfly just out of his cocoon
Or an astronaut walking on the moon.
It's like a beggar finding fortune and fame
Or a loser winning his very first game.

Freedom is a sinner washed in the blood
Or a man turning from evil to good.
It's like when I was forgiven all sin
Or when my heart was changed from within.

Freedom therefore is a state of mind
Or when you are no longer confined.
It's being free to do God's will for you
Or knowing He will see you through.

My Grace is Sufficient

I don't feel like I'm able
I don't feel qualified to serve
I'm a weak and lowly sinner
And His love I don't deserve.

He said:
My strength is made perfect in weakness
My grace is sufficient for thee
Therefore I will boast of my infirmities
That the power of Christ may rest on me.

There are others who could do it
Much better than I ever could
They are much more qualified
His reason I've never understood.

He said:
My strength is made perfect in weakness
My grace is sufficient for thee
Therefore I will boast of my infirmities
That the power of Christ may rest on me.

God's Love

Love ultimately comes from God
It's unconditional and it's free
It was love not the nails
That held Him to that tree.

Jesus came to show us His great love
As on the cross He bled and died
His life became a sacrifice
For you and me He was crucified.

Love isn't meant to be kept inside
It is meant to be shared
We are to love one another
And act like we really cared.

Only our Father in Heaven above
Can truly fill us up inside
He fills our cups with His love
Until love spills over the side.

The Lamb of God

Jesus the worthy Lamb of God
Came to take on the sins of man
The Spirit descended upon Him
He was part of Salvation's plan
He came as a babe in a manger
The product of the virgin birth
To save the souls of many
Was why He came to earth
His life became a sacrifice
As He died for you and me
It was because of His great love
That He came to set us free
Now the perfect Lamb of God
In Heaven sits upon a throne
Holy, holy, holy is He
And worthy is He alone.

O the Passion of Christ

O the passion of Jesus my Lord
Whose love is greater than any sword.
O His faithfulness to the end
As He laid down His life for His friend.
O the beating that Jesus took
His body trembled and it shook.
O the pain He must have felt
With each blow that was dealt.
O the agony as He died
On the cross was crucified.
O the love He had for me
Was what held Him to that tree.
O the blood that was applied
As the spear pierced His side.
O the sin it washed away
It's still sufficient to this day.

Resurrection

At the break of dawn
On that resurrection morning
The women came weeping
It was Jesus they were mourning.
Approaching the tomb in great agony
They saw the stone was rolled away.
Seeing the gardener standing near by
They asked him where Jesus lay.
Why do you search among the dead
Jesus is not here said he.
He broke the chains of death
And rose to set us free.
Now He sits upon His throne
Beside the Father up above.
He intercedes for you and me
And whispers to us words of love.

Love Blooms

Love begins as a tiny sprout
It emerges from the seed that's sown
Taking root within the heart
Growing wherever it is blown.

Love is tender as a fragile shoot
Pushing through the hard spring soil
Then growing stronger day by day
As in this life it must toil.

Love begins to grow small buds
And then blossoms begin to appear
Until love is in full bloom
And continues to bloom year after year.

Love produces tiny seeds
To spread more love all around
Seeds are gently and quietly sent
They land in your heart without a sound.

The Garden of My Heart

To plant the garden of my heart
Preparing the soil is where we start
First we till to loosen the ground
Removing any rocks that may be found
We must decide what we will grow
For we will reap what we sow
As we plant we must beware
Seeds must be planted with great care
As I wait for the seeds to sprout
I must watch and keep varmints out
When the plants begin to grow
Weeds come up in every row
I must pull each and every one
Making sure the plants get lots of sun
Lots of water is also a must
God provides that I trust
Now with proper care of my field
A bountiful crop it will yield
What kind of fruit does your heart produce?
Is it any good or is it of no use?

My Father's Hand

He gently leads me by the hand
In the way I should go.
He doesn't push and shove me,
But encourages me to grow.

He guides me by His great wisdom,
each and every day.
Instilling in my heart and soul,
The need to come and pray.

He heals me with the loving touch,
Of His mighty, powerful hand.
Sometimes His way of healing,
Is not what I had planned.

He protects me beneath His mighty wings,
He sends His angels to surround.
I put my faith and trust in Him,
Knowing His angels are all around.

My Father's Hand (Cont.)

He comforts me in His loving arms,
And tenderly holds me in His embrace.
He kisses away the hurts and pain,
And wipes the tears from my face.

He chastens me with the rod of correction,
When I step out on my own.
He brings me back into His will,
Showing me I can't do it alone.

He delivers me from evil's path,
When temptations come my way.
Giving me another way out,
And bringing me back when I go astray.

My Father's hand is able,
Let's keep it in perspective.
His hand is loving and gentle,
But it's also powerful and effective.

Sweetheart

Sweetheart, you're the love of my life.
I've never regretted becoming your wife.
And though the road is sometimes rough,
Knowing you love me has been enough.
You've stood by me through thick and thin,
No matter how hard it has been.
Sometimes I marvel at the thought,
That God had us together brought.
He knew we were perfectly mated,
For by Him we were created.
He gave us three blessings to share.
To nurture and train, to love and to care.
I thank God for bringing me you.
If I had a choice, I'd still say, "I do".
The years are swiftly slipping away,
Let's make the most of every day.
I promise to love you forevermore,
No matter what God brings our way.
And in His love I will abide,
With you standing by my side.

Mothers

Mothers are a gift from above
They're the perfect example of God's love
For no one can take it away
Her love is forever with us to stay
Distance and time cannot erase
The tenderness and love in a Mother's face
And whether she lives near or far
The door to her heart is always ajar
Even when she's dead and gone
The sweet memory of her love lingers on
Who ever does more for others
Than our own unselfish Mothers
She toils each day for you and me
She's right there when we skin our knee
And when our hearts break in two
She's right there to see us through
Her love is our strength and our guide
Her memory like a light shining inside
She never asks a thing in return
But our love she certainly does earn

The Storms of Life

When the winds of trials
And dark clouds of despair
Come raging into my life
And I feel torn beyond repair.
When the sea of grief
And great waves of sorrow
Threaten to overcome me
And I see no light for tomorrow.

Jesus is my refuge and strength,
The wind and sea obey His voice.
He is the peace in the midst of my storm.
When I put my faith and trust in Him.

Just as the disciples
Out on the stormy sea
Saw their need of Jesus
"Master, save us was their plea"
I cannot do it on my own
I need to come to Him in prayer,
Let Him calm the storms within
And rest in His loving care.

The Storms of Life (cont.)

Jesus is my refuge and strength
The wind and sea obey His voice
He is the peace in the midst of my storm
When I put my faith and trust in Him.

After the storm clouds roll away
And the sea is calm again
The sun comes shining through
And dries up all the rain.
A beautiful and glorious rainbow
In the sky above
Gives us a golden promise
Of His everlasting love.

Jesus is my refuge and strength
The wind and the sea obey His voice.
He is the peace in the midst of my storm
When I put my faith and trust in Him.

Lord You Are My Rock

Chorus:
O Lord, You are the Rock
That my life is anchored to,
O Lord, You are my Rock
You are my peace within.

Your blood has washed me clean
And by your stripes I'm healed
You paid the price for me
And now to You I belong.

You saved me by Your grace
For all eternity
You came into my heart
And from sin set me free.

Lord Jesus, You're my Rock
You're my everything
You've been a friend to me
You love me unconditionally

I Need You Lord

I need Your love to see me through
Your guiding hand to cling to
Your light to shine for me the way
That I might keep from going astray.

Chorus:
O Lord, You are so dear to me
I could not go on without Thee
I know that You died for my sake
I thank You with each breath I take.

I need Your blood to cover me
Your truth from sin to set me free
I need Your peace within my soul
To calm the storms and make me whole.

I need Your mercy and Your grace
As I run life's final race
And as I draw my final breath
To carry me through the door of death.

O Lord Hear My Cry

Ps. 88

O Lord, God of my Salvation
I have cried out day and night
Let my prayer come before You
Incline Your ear to my cry.

For my soul is full of troubles
And my life draws near to the grave
I am counted with those who go down
I am like a man who has no strength.

O Lord, God of my Salvation
I have cried out day and night
Let my prayer come before You
Incline Your ear to my cry.

Lord, I have called upon You daily
I have stretched out my hands to You
I have bowed on bended knee
But Lord, I will wait upon Thee.

O Lord, God of my Salvation
I have cried out day and night
Let my prayer come before You
Incline Your ear to my cry.

The Lord is My Shepherd

Ps 23

The Lord is my Shepherd
He sees to my every need
He gently leads me by the hand
Resting in green grassy meadows
And strolling beside clear crystal streams.

When my heart is hurting and sad inside
He gently comforts me and fills my heart with joy
He leads me down the righteous path
He doesn't push or pull me along
But gently beckons me to come.

Even when we come to a valley
That scares me half to death
The Lord again takes my hand
And the fear is gone as I cling to Him
His rod and staff comforting me again.

He prepares a feast just for me
Where those who wish to harm me can see
He anoints my head with oil
My heart is so full of joy
His mercy is with me and I will dwell with Him forever.

The Journey

Our journey here below
Is just for a period of time
It's like a dress rehearsal
Where we practice our lines
We're not meant here to stay
We are preparing for a better place
So keep your eyes up ahead
On the finish line at the end of this race
God has a plan for each of us
He shapes us into vessels He can use
He has a use for every pot
Even those that are cracked and bruised
He refines us in the fire
With trials He brings our way
They are meant to strengthen us
As we come to Him and pray
If the going was always easy
We would have no need of Him
But when we stumble and fall
He picks us up and sets us on our feet again.

Search My Heart, O God

Search my heart O God
And see if there be any sin
Cleanse my heart, O God
And make me pure within.

You are my Deliverer
I am the slave
You've come to set me free
And my poor soul to save.

Restore my heart, O God
And make me ever new
Shape my heart, O God
And make me just like You.

You are my Deliverer
I am the slave
You've come to set me free
And my poor soul to save.

Prayer

Prayer is a wonderful thing,
When to the Lord our cares we bring.
He's there to listen to our every need,
When to His Word we will heed.
No worry is for Him too small,
To Him we need to take our all.
With God's Love, Mercy, and Grace,
Today's trials we're able to face.
We lift to Him friends so dear,
That He may comfort and draw them near.
Oh, what joy in our heart,
When from sin we depart.
We never know when our time is here,
Dear friend remember it is drawing near.
We do not know how much time we have,
Now is the time our souls to save.
Admitting we're sinners is where we start,
Then inviting the Lord Jesus into our heart.
Oh what joy and peace within,
When we are forgiven from our sin.
Before on someone else we start,
We ask the Lord to search our own heart.
To see if there's some unforgiven sin
Buried deep, deep within.
How can we in Heaven live,
When there's someone we cannot forgive.
We give the Glory to the Lord above,
When our prayers are answered in love.

God's Word

God's Word is a light to my path,
And a lamp to my feet.
It's sharper than any sword,
And a tool in the enemies defeat.

God's Word pierces the heart,
Dividing even the joints and marrow.
It sets the captives free,
And brings comfort to hearts in sorrow.

God's Word is always true,
It's powerful and effective.
It guides our very lives,
And helps us keep an eternal perspective.

God's Word was in the beginning,
And will stand for all eternity.
It came to earth and became flesh,
That we might have victory.

Jesus My Healer

Jesus, You are my Healer,
You healed my broken heart.
You mended the rips and tears,
And put together pieces broken apart.

Jesus, You are my Healer,
You healed my body of cancer.
You put Your hand upon me,
And my prayers did answer.

Jesus, You are my Healer,
You healed my heart of sin.
You shed Your precious blood
And cleansed me from within.

Jesus, You are my Healer,
You healed me through and through.
You took my punishment for me,
And made my life brand new.

Springtime in the Heart

Spring is a time of new life.
When animals and birds have their young.
When flowers and trees begin to bud,
And our life in Christ has begun.

Spring is a time to return to life.
Dormant trees become green once more,
And migrating birds come back again.
When the dead in heart, Christ does restore.

Spring is a time for new growth.
God sends the sun and the rain,
And to our hearts, His Holy Spirit,
To make everything new again.

Spring is a time that comes every year,
And so our hearts need to be reviewed.
To return once more to our first love.
And let our hearts be renewed.

A Rainbow

A beautiful and glorious rainbow
In the sky above,
Reminds us of God's promises,
And of His undying love.

We cannot have a rainbow,
Without first having rain.
Just as we can't receive God's comfort,
Until we experience some pain.

The significance of a rainbow,
Shows us God's Mercy and Grace.
He will strengthen and guide us,
In whatever trials we face.

So when you see a rainbow
Let it speak to your heart.
That God loves and cares for you,
And has from the very start.

Father I Need You

My Father in Heaven above,
Let me hide beneath Your wing.
I rest in Your shadow,
And my cares to You I bring.

Father, I long to hear Your voice,
Whisper peace to my weary soul.
I long to feel Your loving arms,
Comforting me and making me whole.

Father, I bare my heart before You,
I pray search me from within.
Apply the blood You shed,
And cleanse me from all sin.

Father, I need Your Word of Truth
To set my spirit free.
So expose the lies within me,
And cause this blind girl to see.

Revival

Anoint this service, Lord
And revive our hearts I pray.
Send Your Holy Spirit
And leave Him here to stay.

We need to be renewed
And set our eyes on You.
When our priorities are right
Your commands we will do.

Revival begins in our heart
As we seek you, Lord.
Sins are revealed by Your Spirit
And by Your Holy Word.

You are faithful and just
To forgive us for our sin.
When we repent and confess
You wash us pure within.

Restore us to our first love
And put in our hearts a fire.
Give us a burden for the lost
Is our deepest heart's desire.

Cancer of the Heart

There are hundreds of kinds of cancer
And many ways it starts.
The oldest and most common kind
Is cancer of the heart.
It starts out very small
And grows at variable speeds.
It becomes more and more aggressive
As on your heart it feeds.
If you are having symptoms
Of this terrible disease,
Check with the great Physician
And have it diagnosed, please.
It spreads if left untreated,
And causes great agony.
Jesus Christ is the only cure,
His blood the chemo-therapy.
To begin your treatment,
If you've been diagnosed with this cancer,
Take it to the cross of Calvary,
For Jesus Christ is your answer.

Knee-Mail

In this ever changing world
There are many kinds of transportation
And year after year we find
Faster ways of communication.
Telephone replaces telegraph
And snail-mail is replaced by e-mail
But nothing can take the place
Of good old-fashioned knee-mail
There are no internal errors
Or any messages unread
For God answers each and every one
Not our way, but His instead
So even the modern technology
Of this world here below
Can't measure up to God's
When on our knees we go.

To Access Your Knee-mail Account

Be sure you are plugged in
To the only source of power
You must have Jesus installed
To be able to open this file
No updates are required
There is only one version
Enter username and password
To login at anytime
Have Jesus scan your heart-drive
For viruses that will corrupt
He deletes any sin He detects
Before it damages other files
You may now begin downloading
All the blessings God has in store
You may save them to your heart-drive
But be sure to save in thankful mode
You may post your cares on His site
Upload them through your knee-mail
You may find His web address at:
· www.God.com/toHiminprayer.

The Living Water

There's a void within each one of us
And this void we long to fill
We settle for less than the best
When we settle for money or a thrill
We seek after food and fun
We look for fortune and fame
And when this does not fulfill
Well, someone else is to blame
You really can't expect much else
After all that I've been through
I continue to have this unquenchable thirst
I really don't know what to do
That's when Jesus offered me water
Living water for my thirsty soul
It filled my every longing
Quenched my thirst and made me whole
Jesus is the fountain of Living Water
A well that never runs dry
When you are hungry or thirst
He hears your desperate heart's cry.

The Living Stream

The soothing sound of a rippling brook
Is music to my troubled soul
The busyness of a hectic day
On me has taken its toll
As I lay in peaceful bliss
And drink in the sounds of the air
I know without a shadow of doubt
That the Lord truly does care
As my heart dwells on Him
I feel His peace and His love
I sense His very presence
As He reaches down from above
I pour my heart out before Him
And ask Him to fill me up
The blessings and joy spill over the side
As the Lord fills my empty cup
My heart was so lonely and empty inside
I never did consider or even dream
That Jesus would fill me
From His own Living Stream.

Thanksgiving

Thanksgiving is the time of year,
To think of friends and loved ones dear.
We gather together to eat lots of food,
And everyone is in a festive mood.
It really makes me wonder why,
After eating all the turkey and pie,
People tend to forget the real reason,
We are celebrating this Holiday season.
Thanksgiving seems to be forgotten,
In the mad rush of Christmas shopping.
The ghosts and witches of Halloween,
Are replaced by a white wintry scene.
With Santa and his tiny reindeer,
Before Thanksgiving is even here.
We have so much to be thankful for,
All the blessings God has in store.
We have once again been blessed,
With another bountiful harvest.
We have lots of family and friends,
And God's wonderful love that never ends.
So this Thanksgiving let's give it some thought,
Of all the things, be thankful we ought.

A Thankful Heart

A thankful heart is a joyful heart,
And is thankful in all things.
No matter what the circumstances,
Praises to God it continually brings.

A thankful heart is a peaceful heart,
And is trusting at all times.
No matter the size of the issue,
Trusting Him with hundreds and dimes.

A thankful heart is a loving heart,
And is loving to all man.
No matter how much it's been hurt,
Passing on the love inside is its plan.

A thankful heart is a grateful heart,
And is thankful to the One.
No matter that it wasn't deserved,
Seeing all that He has done.

What Does My Life Portray

Can people see Jesus in me
Can they tell I've been set free
Does my life so shine
That they know Christ is mine
Does it show by the way I live
And do I others freely forgive
In all things do I portray
And point others toward the Way
Do I do all that I can
To win the favor of man
Or do I fear the God above
And witness to others in love
To those around, how do I look
Do I live according to the Book
For Jesus is coming back you see
He's coming back for you and me
May I then in Him be found
He'll lift me up to higher ground
May He then say, "Well done
Thou good and faithful servant, come".

My Heavenly Home

I'm going to a faraway land
A land where there is no night.
To a city in the sky above
Where God Himself is the light.
A mansion is prepared for me
And the streets are laid with gold.
Nothing there is measured by time
A place where no one grows old.
We will worship the mighty King
And there we will reign with Him.
The angel choir their praises sing
And their voices never grow dim.
The saints are bowing before the throne
Casting their crowns on the glassy sea.
Jesus is waiting at the pearly gate
Waiting to open the gate for me.
Oh what a glorious day that will be
When I cross to the other side.
I'm welcomed to my home in the sky
For eternity with Jesus to abide.

A Friend

A friend is someone who loves you,
No matter what you've done.
They stick closer than a brother,
When their trust you have won.

A friend is someone who stands by you,
When everyone else has fled.
They stay right by your side,
No matter what others have said.

A friend is someone who knows you,
And still loves you anyway.
They overlook your faults,
And don't let them get in the way.

A friend is someone who cares,
And sticks with you to the end.
No greater love has any man,
Than to lay down his life for his friend.

A friend is someone who will die for you,
And that's just what Jesus did.
He gave His life on Calvary,
And paid the price He bid.

Peace

When peace like a river
Flows deep within my soul.
I feel loved and secure
And my heart is made whole.
The river begins in Jesus Christ
And it spills out into my life.
It tumbles down o'er rocks and cliffs
Washing away the raw edges of strife.
Peace washes over me
And calms my troubled heart.
It soothes and restores my spirit
And keeps me from falling apart.
It floods the valley that I'm in
Filling a dry and thirsty land.
Like a spring in the desert
Flowing on without end.
Peace transcends all understanding
And by God is given.
Without this peace in my soul
It's hard to go on livin'.

Starry Skies

Staring up at a star filled sky
On a bright moon-lit night.
As I gaze at the heavens above
I behold the wondrous sight.
I am totally in awe
That God named each and every one
And He created them all
The same day He made the sun.
He must have taken a handful of diamonds
And tossed them into the sky.
For they twinkle and they shine
Down upon us from on high.
I wonder how many there are
And how God put each in place.
Only God knows the mysteries
Of all that's in outer space.

I Shall Not Be Moved

When I stand firm in Him
I shall not be moved.
When I put my trust in Him
I will not be shaken.
When I stand on the solid Rock
I shall not be swayed.
When I am anchored in Him
I will not drift away.
When my feet are planted
I shall not be uprooted.
When I stand on the Word of God
I will not be easily deceived.
When I am set free by Truth
I shall not be bound.
When I am in tune with God
I will not be off key.
When I put my faith in God
I shall have no faith in myself.

I Surrender All

Chorus:
Oh, my God, I surrender all.
To You my Lord, I give my all.
I put my life into Your hands, O Lord.
From this day on, I surrender all to You.

~~~

I give my hands in service to You, Lord.
I give my feet to walk with You all day.
I give my lips to spread the Gospel News.
I give my heart to love and to be loved by You.

~~~

Oh, my God, I surrender all.
To You my Lord, I give my all.
I put my life into Your hands, O Lord.
From this day on, I surrender all to You.

The Joy of The Lord is Your Strength

Chorus:
The joy of the Lord is your strength.
The joy of the Lord is your strength.
He should be high and lifted up.
So shout to the Lord with all your might
And sing praises to His name

When Satan tries to sift you
And you feel like you just can't go on
Just lift up the name of the Lord
And He will see you through.

When you're down in the valley
And you're feeling all blue inside
Just lift up the name of the Lord
And He will see you through.

When anxiety is great within you
And stress is gettin' you down
Just lift up the name of the Lord
And He will see you through.

If you should hear His voice a callin'
O do not harden your heart
Just lift up the name of the Lord
And He will see you through.

Open Up Your Life

Circumstances don't have to hinder us.
We can turn them into a stepping stone.
We need not be overcome by it,
But overcome it through Christ alone

Chorus:
Today He's saying to you:
Don't just open up your heart,
But open up your life as well.
Let Me fill you with My love
And put your trust in Me.

Circumstances are meant to transform us.
Just like the potter does his clay.
So let us recognize the reason
And let God shape us His very own way.

Today He's saying to you:
Don't just open up your heart,
But open up your life as well
Let Me fill you with My love
And put your trust in Me.

Living on Borrowed Time

Time is running out.
Eternity is drawing near.
Jesus may return tonight.
Or it may be next year.
Either way we're running out of time.
We do not know how long.
We must tell others about Jesus,
In word, deed, and song.
Each of us is given time.
Divided into weeks, days, and hours.
The time we have is borrowed.
It really isn't ours.
We must use our time wisely.
We must give an account of our time.
Just as we give an account of our money,
Down to the very last dime.
My plea to you is this:
Remember your time is on loan.
Remember the One who loaned it to you,
And use it for Him alone.

Priceless Treasures

Priceless treasures, value untold
Stored away, memories unfold.
Collected dust over the years
Cherished, but stained with tears.
Love letters tied with a string
Bittersweet memories bring.
White gown of satin and lace
Images of our dear angels face.
A pair of glasses Grandma used to wear
A lock of her curly gray hair.
Grandpa's Bible with well worn pages
Handed down through the ages.
A patchwork quilt stitched with love
Speaks of memories of those gone above.
A dried flower from a big bouquet
Brings memories of a special birthday.
A picture drawn by little hands
Of fairy tales in faraway lands.
These memories of days gone by
Always brings a tear to my eye.

The Freedom Trail

On the road to Breaking Free
Obedience is the key.
Relying on God is a must
Putting in Him our faith and trust.
On our own strength we cannot stand
But walking with Him hand in hand.
Leaning on Him for our every need
Is where we find strength indeed.
As the potter forms the clay
We must allow Him to have His way.
Right from the very start
Surrendering to Him our whole heart.
We find a place of quiet rest
When we have victoriously passed the test
Of surrendering to His will
Then our souls He'll refresh and fill.
His yoke is an easy thing
When to Him our cares we bring.
He says, "Won't you come away with me?
For I have come that you may be free."

Sitting At Jesus' Feet

That place of quiet rest
At my Jesus' feet
Has become so dear to me
And ever so sweet.

As I bask there in peace
And soak up His love
I sense the pleasure
Of my Father up above.

It touches my very heart
And soothes my weary soul
To know that I'm complete
And in Him I'm whole.

My spirit is refreshed
And I feel brand new
Like the crisp and freshness
Of early morning dew.

May I come here often
At His feet to lay
And take this sweet peace
With me throughout the day.

Rendezvous

Father, I want to bask in Your love
I want to sail on rivers of joy
And swim in pools of peace.
I want to scale the utmost high
And stand on the mountain peak
I want to run in meadows green
And lay beside the still waters
I want to walk hand in hand
And sit low at Your feet
I want to rise on wings of eagles
And float on the clouds above
I want to wade in rippling brooks
And splash in streams of mercy
I want to stroll along the beach
With You by my side
I want to walk in the early morning
As the sun begins to rise
I want to sit and watch
As You paint the eastern skies.
Father, I want to come away with You
And spend some quality time.

The Lighthouse

A beautiful lighthouse on the shore
Stands tall beside a stormy sea.
It's light a beacon in the night
Guiding the ships out at sea.
The glowing light beckons to all
And when the ships are lost at sea
This guiding light shines the way.
It keeps many ships from crashing
Into the reef along the shore.
Without the light burning inside
This lighthouse is only a building
And the ships are lost as can be.
We are this lighthouse
Guiding others by the light inside.
This light is Jesus Christ
And if our light goes out
Where will those lost ships be.
Then we the lighthouse
Will not be serving our purpose
But simply standing beside the sea.

Beauty

Beauty we all long to possess
Physical beauty comes and goes
But true beauty comes from within.
And bursts into bloom just as a rose.
As a flower cannot contain its perfume
So our hearts cannot contain its joy.
A new mother beholds her child
Beautiful to her whether girl or boy.
Christ beholds us, His virgin bride
He beholds our beauty within.
For we were made beautiful
When He cleansed us from sin.
When we surrender our lives to Him
We are made in His image.
And as grapes made into wine
Beauty deepens as we age.
Beauty lies in the eyes of the beholder
And Christ does behold His bride.

Searching

I had a void deep in my heart
It was meant for Jesus from the start.
I tried to fill that void within
But ended up deep in sin.

I tried to fill it with lots of fun
I even thought I needed more sun.
Then I tried some alcohol
Which really didn't help at all.

The void seemed to grow bigger still
Until at times I felt quite ill.
There was this emptiness deep within
And I was sinking deeper in sin.

When I reached the end of my rope
Jesus came and He gave me hope.
Nothing else could fill me up
Only Jesus could fill my cup.

On the cross Jesus died
For you and me was crucified.
He left His mansion up above
Came down to show us His great love.

Longing of My Heart

I have a longing in my heart
My Jesus more fully to know.
To walk hand in hand with Him
And go with Him wherever He may go.

~~~

Jesus held out His hand
And said "Come away with Me."
Walking hand in hand with Jesus
My spirit's been set free.

~~~

I have a longing in my heart
To walk with Him each day.
To walk hand in hand with Him
And in His presence ever stay.

~~~

Jesus held out His hand
And said "Come away with Me."
Walking hand in hand with Jesus
My spirit's been set free.

The Lord My Guide

Father give me peace, give me love
Help my mind on You to stay.
If I step out of Your will
Pull me back without delay.
You know my thoughts O Lord
And You have a plan for me I know.
You give me mountain top experiences
Then take me to the valley to grow.
You love me with an unconditional love
And You have my best interest at heart.
You care about the little things in my life
And You have from the very start.
You gave Your Son to die for me
When I was still deep in sin.
His precious blood was shed
That I might be pure within.
Father I cannot crucify the flesh alone
I can only surrender it to You.
Fill me with Your Spirit of Truth
And give me strength in all I do.
Father I rely on You for all
To get me through the day.
Your Truth and Your Word
To guide me in Your Way.

Cup of Praise

Jesus, may You enjoy the rich aroma
As I pour my praise unto You.
May You savor the sweet taste
Of all the glory and honor due.

Jesus, may my praise be music to Your ears
As I praise You with my lips.
May my praises ring for You alone
As I touch Your scars with fingertips.

Jesus, You are the worthy Lamb of God
To whom all praise is given.
You alone are the reason
That I can go on livin'

Walk in the Spirit

The fruit of the spirit is love
So love your neighbor as yourself.
The joy of the Lord is your strength
So be filled with joy unspeakable.
Peace is a gift from God
So accept your gift by faith in Him.
Patience is a virtue
So bear fruit with patience.
God's merciful kindness is great toward us
So show kindness to Your brother.
Surely goodness and mercy follow me
So abound in goodness always.
Great is the faithfulness of the Lord
So be faithful in all you do.
Jesus was full of lowliness and gentleness
So let your gentleness be known to all.
Self-control is the very best way to go
So you best control yourself.
Now these are the fruits of the Spirit
So you do well to walk in them.

Seeking God's Will

Father, I seek to know Your will
And the way You would have me go.
Speak to my heart, O Lord
And guide my steps that I may know.

Father, I know Your will is best for me
So I surrender my will to You.
I know You have a plan and purpose
And I trust You will see me through.

Father, show me which way I should go
And which road I should take.
It's a difficult situation we're in
When our livelihood is at stake.

Father, give me peace within
Knowing You will work it out.
And when it's all over
I wonder what I worried about.

Peaceful Moments

I sit quiet moments with the Lord to share
Drinking sights and sounds of the morning air
Singing of the birds is music to my ears
Sun peeping over the horizon brings tears
Stillness disrupted as a car passes by
Disturbed birds take to the sky
In a flash the moment has passed
If peaceful moments like these could only last.

The Steadfast Mind

Satan fights on the battlefield of the mind
Searching for some weakness to find.
He's seeking whom he may devour
But over the Christian he has no power.
So he came up with a back-up plan
To deceive with lies the mind of man.
Sometimes he comes like a roaring lion
Other times twisting the truth and lyin'.
If he can cause me to stumble
Then down my faith will tumble.
I can be held captive by those lies
Not knowing God's truth it defies.
A healthy mind is constantly active
A healthy spirit takes every thought captive.
The truth that I receive
Can set me free from the lies I believe.
It will set my spirit free
When my mind is steadfast in Thee.

Little Country Church

The little country church
Stands tall and proud
Light spilling from her windows
The cobblestone path inviting
Drawing me to a closer look
Charming steeple
Points to the sky
As if to point to the One
Sitting on His throne
The door compels me to open
And come inside a spell
The soft light from the window
Draws me like a moth to flame
I can't seem to stop myself
Opening the door I peer inside
Soft light beckons me
Peace draped about
Feelings of love wash over me
As I stand gazing in awe
At the scene before my eyes
A rugged cross empty and tall
Three rusty nails covered with blood
A spear and a crown of thorns
Laying at the foot of the cross
Falling to my knees
I know why I have come.

Shattered Dream

A little dream is born
It grows and tries out its wings
It flies unhindered in the sky
Like an eagle soaring overhead
Whirling and twirling it flew about
Day by day it continued to soar
Until one day it fell with a thud
It is bruised but still alive
Someone walking, unknowingly steps on it
Shattering it into a million pieces
A little dream dies.